A

Breaking Free of the You They want you to Be

Free to Be Me

1st Edition

Dr. T. Nichole Spies, LMFT, MS, NBCC, Dmin

INTRODUCTION

Have you ever found yourself in a place where you were not sure of yourself, or found yourself always on a mission to please others and in return found yourself sad and unfulfilled in your life? Have you ever found yourself questioning your worth and if you had what it takes to really be your authentic self without worrying what others thought? Struggling with life and trying to figure out who you are can be frustrating and sometimes even depressing.

In this guide you will find a blueprint to help you break free from the grips of living a life based on the image you see of yourself that others have created of you. Over the next 21 days you will learn to love yourself and begin to walk in the image of the person that you desire to be. Each chapter will provide you with practical techniques to help you

2

move toward the person you desire to be. You will also find at the end of each chapter prompts to help you navigate the journey of rewriting your story that will lead you to that person who is fighting to break through. Allow yourself to be opened to change and take your time to complete each day's Work. There is a 21-day Journal in the back of the book to provide you space to continue your journey.

While on your journey to be who you were destined to be, allow yourself to be okay with choosing you. Many have been taught to be selfless and always put others before themselves, but do not get caught up in the misconception that this means at the cost of losing yourself to make them happy. Free yourself from the guilt of not meeting the expectations of being the person that other people want you to be. Being true to yourself is the most important part of this entire journey. You must be happy with what you want and not with pleasing the rest of the world. There will always be people standing in judgment, but you must choose you.

Choosing you means learning how to love and accept yourself as you are. Loving yourself means that anything that you are not happy with in your life you can change it. This change is for you and not to fit the mold that other people want you to fit. Self-love and self-discovery go hand in hand, because to be successful on this journey of "Free to be Me," you must allow yourself to experience those two elements to achieve maximum growth. Open your heart and your mind as you begin this journey of freeing yourself and breaking free from the you, they want you to be and becoming the person you desire to be.

Are you ready to become who you want to be and stop living this version of your life that does not speak to the truth of who you are? Are you ready to be empowered, to say no more will I drain myself trying to keep up with this false image to fit their mold? Are you ready to move from living to please others and not please yourself? Well, if you have answered yes to either of these questions, then you are already making progress toward your goal of becoming your authentic self. It is time for you to take the next steps to becoming a happier you.

WEEK ONE

Week One

WHERE THE JOURNEY BEGINS

The fact is that many individuals have taken on the identity or narrative in their minds of who or how others see them. If you find yourself in this place, then let us start on your road to breaking free from all that keeps you stuck in that place. Moving from the place of being sad to make others happy is crucial to your journey. It is your time to step into the light and free yourself from those who have held you captive, voiding your identity.

Remove the mask created for you by your family, friends, partner, job, and society. Grab hold of the reality of your true identity and embrace the journey to your true freedom. Letting go of this image that shields who you are can be a challenge, but you already have in you what you need to shatter it into pieces. Once this mask is shattered do not collect the pieces but destroy them because your goal is never to become that person again. What you need now is just the desire and will to begin.

Now is your time to break free from the you they want you to be and evolve into your own person. You can chart your own path without getting permission from anyone else on the direction of your life and who you should be in it. Right now, you may not believe it, but you need to know and accept that you are an amazing, smart, strong, and important individual. You are worth more than the value others have tried to place on you all these years.

It is time to shift your thinking so that not only will you know who you are authentically, but you will reclaim the power over your identity and feel empowered to walk in your truth. It is your time to step into the light and free yourself from those who have held you captive, voiding your true identity.

Day One

"Life is full of expectations, but when I allow the expectations of others to control who I am I lose who I am meant to be."

Let us begin to explore how you got to where you are today regarding how you see yourself. Here you will use the prompts to help you identify where you begin conforming into a mold that was not your true identity.

Do The Work

Where did the idea of who you are originate?

_____

_____

_____

_____

_____

When did you first start conforming to who others thought you should be:

_____

_____

_____

_____

_____

What are the images others have created for you?

_____

_____

_____

_____

_____

"I AM FREE TO BE ME"

What does being free to be me mean to you:

_____

_____

_____

_____

_____

Week One

Day Two

"Becoming who I want to be begins with a shift in what I think"

Stepping into your true self begins with shifting the narrative about how you view yourself. If you have spent your life living according to the box others have put you in has become a part of how you see yourself. Some of what you see you may like and some of what you see may be exhausting. It is up to you how you shift your thinking to change that narrative.

You have the opportunity today to rewrite your story according to how you see it. You have the power to shift your thinking from where it is now to how you would like to think moving forward. One way to begin shifting your thinking is by identifying the beliefs that do not resonate with you because they were placed there by others.

Do The Work

What is the narrative that others have created for you that you want to escape?

_____

_____

_____

_____

_____

What part of the narrative that others have created for you do you want to hold onto?

_____

_____

_____

_____

_____

How do I see myself?

_____

_____

_____

_____

_____

"Today I choose to allow myself to shift my mindset to fit the narrative I want and not what others have created for me."

What does shifting to a new mindset look like to you:

_____

_____

_____

Day Three

"Removing the mask can be scary, but I have to do it to discover who I truly am."

Masks are used to hide our true identity. Sometimes we use masks to create an image that we think that society wants to see of us. Sometimes we use a mask because we do not like what we see when we remove it because we do not think others will be as accepting when we have it on. No matter why the mask is there, it still hides the true identity of who you are, but do not be afraid to embrace who you are beneath the mask. The person you are beneath that mask is an amazing and formidable individual, you just must believe it.

Do The Work

What does the mask that you have created to fit in with others look like?

_____

_____

_____

_____

_____

What fears come to mind when you think about removing the mask:

_____

_____

_____

_____

_____

What do you think of the person behind the mask?

_____

_____

_____

_____

_____

_____

TODAY'S AFFIRMATION

"Who I am is worthy, therefore making me good enough"

List five wonderful things about yourself that

contribute to your worth:

_____

_____

_____

_____

_____

19

Day Four

"The direction of one's life is determined by the vision they possess inside their mind."

We all have a destiny and we all can have obstacles that try to detour our paths. These detours can be in the form of the opinions of others, the expectations others have set for us, and even our own doubt to reach our destiny based on those aforementioned factors. However, our destiny can only be stopped if we allow the opinion and expectations of others to cause us to abort it. Therefore, we must look within to our own truth and allow our vision to flourish. It takes making up your mind to give yourself permission to dream big and conquer the fear of the success that can stop us from the life we were destined to achieve.

Do The Work

What or who in your past has been the obstacle that has detoured you from reaching your destiny:

_____

_____

_____

_____

_____

How has this obstacle impacted your view of yourself?

_____

_____

_____

_____

_____

When you think about your destiny what do you envision for yourself:

_____

_____

_____

_____

_____

"I Determine my destiny according to the goals I have set for MYSELF"

List the top five goals you have set for yourself to accomplish:

_____

_____

_____

_____

_____

Week One

Day Five

"Living Life unapologetically for myself is the best choice for my happiness"

Living your life for you can release you from the pressure of performing for others. Learning to be intentional about living life on your own terms can relieve you of unnecessary stress as well as the pressure to be perfect to be accepted by others. We all have a desire to be accepted by others at some point in our lives but is it worth it when this type of thinking causes you to forfeit your own happiness.

It is important that on your journey to be free that you live life by choosing you and not allow yourself to be left out. So, allow yourself the space to live life and do the things you enjoy. Make the choices that work for you and not others.

Do The Work

What happiness have you forfeited to make others
happy:

_____

_____

_____

_____

_____

When you chose to make others happy over yourself
how did that make you feel:

_____

_____

_____

_____

_____

Describe what it will look like when you begin to choose things that make you happy:

_____

_____

_____

_____

_____

TODAY'S AFFIRMATION

"Today I choose to make myself happy"

List five things that you can do today to make YOU happy:

_____

_____

_____

_____

_____

Day Six

"Being true to myself may cause others discomfort, but not being true to who I am will causes me agony"

Many have been taught to live a selfless life, always putting others before ourselves. When we think about that statement what does that really mean. I think that many have confused putting others before ourselves, because when this is practiced, we tend to put ourselves on the back burner. Being selfless does not mean that we dismiss who we are to make other people happy, it means that we do not step on other people for our own gain or selfish ambitions. It is okay to make yourself a priority.

Do The Work

Who did you make happy and in the process of it made yourself sad:

_____

_____

_____

_____

_____

What was it that you did to please them?

_____

_____

_____

_____

_____

In that moment what did you want to do that would have been true to yourself:

_____

_____

_____

_____

_____

TODAY'S AFFIRMATION

"I will not be sad at the risk of denying who I am to make others happy"

Describe what today's affirmation means to you:

_____

_____

_____

Week One

Day Seven

"Accepting me as I am, is embracing all of me with confidence"

When you choose to embrace all of who you are, you must do the work to rid your thinking of all the negative things and comments of others that have infiltrated your thinking or perception of who you are. Working free from the thought of you based on how others have influenced your thinking is not always easy but is always doable. You must give yourself permission to be the you that you want to be.

You must determine in your mind that you will not cheat yourself of the opportunity to be who you truly are. Be confident in the person you are and allow room for that vision to grow.

Do The Work

What are some of the thoughts you have about who you are that bring down your confidence:

_____

_____

_____

_____

_____

Based on your previous answer to the question above what is a new thought about yourself to counteract the old thought:

_____

_____

_____

_____

_____

31

What steps will you take moving forward to help you build your confidence in who you are:

_____

_____

_____

_____

_____

TODAY'S AFFIRMATION

"Today I choose to love who I am and the person I will become on my self-discovery journey"

Describe what your discovery journey of self looks like to you:

_____

_____

_____

WEEK TWO

SELF-DISCOVERY IS THE ROAD TO EMBRACING YOURSELF

When we have spent most of our lives living it according to the expectation of others, we can lose ourselves in that image. Loosing ourselves in that image can cause us to neglect ourselves. It is now time for you to rediscover who you are and what you want from life. Now is not the time to sit in pity over not embracing who you truly are, before now. You are here and that is what counts.

While on this journey it is not uncommon for you to feel emotions of guilt, fear, and anxiety. These feelings are common and brought on by the idea of stepping into who you truly are and not the person others expect you to be. This change takes away the power from those who have tried to keep you in a box. Reclaim your power and put those fear, that guilt, and that anxiety in its place. You now possess all the power over your life.

The only person at this point that can hold you back is you. Remember everything you do from this point forward needs to be intentional as you continue this journey "Free to Be Me." Do not forget to love you, you are the most important person in the room. And since you spend all your time with yourself do not you think it is time that you get to know you. I know this journey can be exhausting, but the reward at the end is so much greater than the struggle.

Day One

"Fear of stepping into my truth will not paralyze me from reaching my destiny"

Fear can be an immensely powerful emotion. Fear has stopped so many in their tracks from reaching their destiny. This fear can come from simply not knowing what people will think of your change or your own personal fear of facing the unknown that the change may bring.

You have nothing to fear when it comes to what other people think because there will always be someone with an opinion on how another person should live their life. So, defeat that fear by telling yourself that you know what is best for your life and that you will live according to what makes you happy. Fear is an illusion to keep you stuck, do not let it win.

Do The Work

What does fear look like to you:

_____

_____

_____

_____

_____

What do you fear the most about being yourself?

_____

_____

_____

_____

_____

What can you do to change that?

_____

_____

_____

_____

_____

"Today I choose to defeat fear and not allow it to paralyze me for reaching my destiny"

Describe how being free of the fear of changing will impact your destiny:

_____

_____

_____

_____

_____

Week Two

Day Two

"Being true to myself releases an endless flow of my true potential"

When you walk in the image of your true self the freedom that will be released will cause you to excel beyond your wildest dream. With this new found freedom your potential is endless. By taking the steps to discover who you really are you will come into the light of not only who you are, but what you want to do, and where you want to go.

Allow yourself to bring those dreams and visions of your life that have been stifled to bloom and flourish. You need to know that you deserve happiness, and that happiness begins within you. Do not be afraid to change, no matter what. You are your own person, be confident in that person.

Do The Work

What are your dreams that you want to pursue?

_____

_____

_____

_____

_____

What fear is holding you back from pursuing your dreams?

_____

_____

_____

_____

_____

What are the steps you need to take to start pursuing your dreams?

_____

_____

_____

_____

_____

"Today I will walk in the full potential of who I am"

How will you walk into your full potential today?

_____

_____

_____

_____

_____

Week Two

Day Three

"Sometimes I have to get out of a place to elevate my space"

There are times when we find ourselves in environments that do not support who we are as a person. That place can be mentally, physically, and even spiritually. It is important that you create an environment that is conducive of who you desire to be. You need to have an eagle's mentality, which means soaring above the chaos that could potentially ground you. See eagles never fly in a storm (chaos) they rise above it to make it to their destination.

So today, purpose in your heart and mind that you are going to rise above people, places, things, and situations that do not help push you

43

toward becoming who you want to be. Remove yourself from those who take from who you are and surround yourself with people who pour into you that help nurture you toward who you are becoming. Most importantly, transform your own headspace. Dismiss the negative images of yourself that have kept you back from reaching your full potential. It is time to elevate and walk in your true purpose and become the you that has been trapped inside.

Do The Work

Who is hindering your elevation?

_____

_____

_____

_____

_____

What thoughts about yourself are keeping you in the chaos?

_____

_____

_____

_____

_____

Write down three new positive thoughts to support

who you want to be:

_____

_____

_____

_____

_____

TODAY'S AFFIRMATION
"Today I choose to free myself of things and people that do not support my journey"

What things and people will you free yourself from that keep you from reaching your full potential?

_____

_____

_____

_____

_____

Week Two

Day Four

"Believing in myself can be a struggle at times, but the struggle is helping me to be my true self"

On this journey of self-discovery one of the hardest things to do is finding the courage to believe in yourself. For so long you may have told yourself that you are not worthy but be encouraged and give yourself permission to know that you are. Life may have thrown some blows to your confidence, and you struggle with believing in yourself, but that is not how your story has to end.

Gold and diamonds go through a process before their true beauty is revealed. Imagine yourself like that diamond or the gold, you may have had to go through extreme pressure or even heat, but you are emerging as something of worth and value. Even the struggle of believing in yourself is helping to shape who you are truly meant to be. Remember this is a process and be patient with your transformation. So, believe in yourself and your ability to be the best version of yourself.

Do The Work

Why do you struggle to believe in myself?

_____

_____

_____

_____

_____

List Three Positive about yourself:

_____

_____

_____

_____

_____

What steps will you take to improve my self-confidence:

_____

_____

_____

_____

_____

TODAY'S AFFIRMATION

"Today I choose to win no matter what life throws my way"

What does today's affirmation mean to you?

_____

_____

_____

_____

_____

Week Two

Day Five

"Learning to love all of who I am is one of the most powerful experiences in the world"

Self-love is something that we all could use a great big dose of. Often in the hustle and bustle of life we spend so much time focused on others that we tend to forget about ourselves. Another component that is important on this journey of self-discovery is learning to love yourself.

Loving who you are despite what anybody else thinks is one of the most important things that you need to remember while on this journey. Do not allow guilt to creep in because you choose yourself for a change. Take some time to love on you, treat yourself, appreciate yourself, and enjoy the experience of falling in love with yourself.

Do The Work

What does self-love look like to you?

_____

_____

_____

_____

_____

Why do you find it hard to love yourself?

_____

_____

_____

_____

_____

How can you show yourself love?

_____

_____

_____

_____

_____

"Today I choose to be intentional about loving who I am in this moment"

What will you do today to show yourself love?

_____

_____

_____

_____

_____

Week Two

Day Six

"Seeing myself for who I am for the first time was truly amazing because of the freedom I felt"

How you see yourself is particularly important on this self-discovery journey. Learning to transform your mindset from embracing how people see you to seeing yourself for who you are brings the sense of freedom that helps to establish your worth. Your worth is not contingent upon what others think or say it is based on how you view yourself. Choosing to accept the best version of yourself based on your own assessment creates confidence and produces power. Your worth is more than mere words; it is the core of who you are and the power in your stride. So, release the freedom that you desire by loving who you see in the mirror.

Do The Work

When you look in the mirror, who do you see?

_____

_____

_____

_____

_____

Is the person you see the person you want to be and why or why not?

_____

_____

_____

_____

_____

What steps can you take to reflect the image you want to see?

_____

_____

_____

_____

_____

"Today I choose to accept me for who I am because I am worthy"

What does today's affirmation mean to you?

_____

_____

_____

_____

_____

Week Two

Day Seven

"Life is full of choices just be sure the ones you are making benefit you"

How many times have you found yourself in a position of making a choice and choosing what you thought others would want you to do? When finding yourself in this place it can be difficult because you want to make others happy. Finding your voice and saying, "No, I'm going to choose what I want," is the first step in freeing yourself from the bondage of people pleasing.

Everyone at one time or another has made choices based on the opinions of others. Moving to a place of independence and being confident will begin to develop as you take the necessary steps in learning to make choices for yourself. It is time for you to stand on your own two feet and trust yourself that the choices you make are the choices that make you happy.

Do The Work

List a choice you have made based on other people's opinions?

_____

_____

_____

_____

_____

How did making that choice make you feel?

_____

_____

_____

_____

_____

If you could go back in time and change that choice, what would you choose?

_____

_____

_____

_____

_____

TODAY'S AFFIRMATION
"Today I choose to make choices that make me happy"

What choices will you make today to promote your happiness?

_____

_____

_____

_____

_____

WEEK THREE

WEEK THREE

The Art of Saying No

Do you ever find yourself doing things that you do not want to do? Do you find yourself wrestling with the thought of saying no to others because you do not want to hurt their feelings? It can really be difficult when it comes to dealing with those that are closest to you, it can be your partner, a family member, or a good friend. Learning the art of saying no just the thought can sometimes bring discomfort. This struggle can be as real as they come, but you can master the art of saying no.

This part of the journey focuses on taking the guilt out of saying no when what they want does not fit who you are. Hopefully by now you have begun to break free from what has been holding you back from being able to be your true self. Are you ready to start saying no and standing your ground when it comes to what is best for developing who you are?

Then do the work and learn the art of saying no.

Week Three

Day One

"Learning to say no frees me from obligations of others that do not fit who I am"

When you decide to say no it is not without its challenges. Often when you decide that saying no is a benefit to yourself, you can feel guilt and that guilt can cause you to give in to the wants of others. Saying no it is not a terrible thing because it offers freedom to be who you want to be. Saying no gives you liberty and helps you avoid the trap of being obligated to do what others want you to do based on their desires and not your own.

On this journey saying no allows you the opportunity to create boundaries that are necessary for your self growth. When you are afraid to say no you will eventually overextend yourself which can lead to burn out. Burn out can leave you unhappy, stressed, and unfulfilled. When you learn to say no you give yourself the ability to be the masters of your own fate. Do not allow the guilt of saying no to stop you from creating necessary boundaries to reach your full potential and to take care of yourself.

Do The Work

List a time you overextended yourself because you did not say no?

_____

_____

_____

_____

_____

Who do you find most challenging to say no to?

_____

_____

_____

_____

_____

How will you practice say no moving forward?

_____

_____

_____

_____

_____

_____

TODAY'S AFFIRMATION
"Today I choose to say no and not feel guilty to the things that do not promote who I want to be"

What steps can you take today to ensure that you do not feel guilty about saying no?

_____

_____

_____

_____

_____

Week Three

Day Two

"Learning to speak my truth gave my voice power"

Succumbing to the expectations of others when you do not say no takes away the power that you should possess. Living life on your own terms and accepting who you are is empowering. It cannot be expressed enough that allowing yourself to say no to people when you do not want to do something is okay.

Walk in your truth. Refuse to compromise who you are by agreeing to every idea of who you are and what you need to do that is imposed by others. Take your power back by standing up for what you want. Reclaim your power and walk in the truth of who you are.

Do The Work

Describe a time when you gave your power away:

_____

_____

_____

_____

_____

What does living life on your own term look like?

_____

_____

_____

_____

_____

List three ways that you can reclaim your power:

_____

_____

_____

_____

_____

TODAY'S AFFIRMATION
"Today I choose to walk in my own truth and reclaim my power"

What truth will you walk in today to reclaim your power?

_____

_____

_____

_____

_____

Week Three

Day Three

"Saying no is not being mean it is choosing what I need opposed to what somebody else wants"

Ignoring your needs will result in neglect. Taking time to practice self-care is not being selfish, it is doing what you need to do to ensure your own well-being. It is important that you create a self-care plan to take care of your mental, physical, and emotional well-being.

Saying no promotes self-care which will lead you down a path of peace and restoration. Doing this helps you make yourself a priority. This can also help in regaining and building your self-confidence. Choosing you does not mean you are ignoring everything and everyone in your life, it means that you have chosen to make yourself happy.

Do The Work

Create a self-care plan for yourself:

_____

_____

_____

_____

_____

_____

_____

_____

_____

_____

_____

_____

_____

_____

"Today I choose to meet my needs and not neglect myself"

What need will you focus on meeting today for yourself?

_____

_____

_____

_____

_____

Week Three

Day Four

"Saying no gives me control of my own life so that I can be free to be me"

Another critical point to learning to say no is that it offers us back control of our lives. When we allow others to dictate to us our every move, we give them absolute control. Remember that the feeling of guilt will try to creep in when you say no to those things that you do not want to do. Moving forward in your journey you must be in control of your own life. No one gets to tell you what to do or how to think.

When we think about freedom it is absolute control to do what we desire and not be dictated or forced into things that we do not want to do. Talking about saying no does not mean that you never say yes it just simply means you get to choose when you say yes. Not every project, function, event, or task is your responsibility. Pick wisely so that you can control your time, your life, and the freedom to be who you are.

Do The Work

Describe a time you did something out of feeling obligated that you had no desire to do:

_____

_____

_____

_____

_____

How did that make you feel?

_____

_____

_____

_____

_____

"Today I choose to take control of my life unapologetically by saying No"

How will you take control of your life today?

_____

_____

_____

_____

_____

Week Three

Day Five

"Saying no is empowering and frees you of the unnecessary stress of others"

Every day we are faced with problems of our own and even sometimes we take on the problems of others. However, when we choose to make other people's problems our problems it creates a plethora of unnecessary stress. We can find ourselves worrying about how to fix other people's issues. When this is done those individuals do not even take an interest in solving their own problems. Why would they try to solve their own problems if you are destined to be the fixer?

It is time for you to stop allowing the stress of others to become your burden. Picking up the pieces of your own life comes with enough stress, therefore when you learn how to release yourself from being responsible for other people's problems you open yourself up once again to be free, it cannot be said enough saying no is freedom, but always saying yes is bondage.

Do The Work

How often do you feel pressured by others to deal with their problems?

_____

_____

_____

_____

_____

How often do you find yourself making others' problems yours?

_____

_____

_____

_____

_____

The next time you feel pressured to make other people problems your what will you do different than before?

_____

_____

_____

_____

_____

"Today I choose not to allow other people's problems to be my issues"

If someone comes to you today with their problems and tries to make them yours, what will be your response?

_____

_____

_____

_____

_____

Week Three

Day Six

"Stop people pleasing and start pleasing by simply saying no"

When we talk about people pleasing there are good and bad aspects of that trait. It is okay to be concerned about others' needs and wants but not to the point where you neglect yourself. People pleasing should never result in you not focusing on the things that make you happy.

If you find that this is a trait you possess you may want to think about your motive for pleasing other people. What is the reasoning for this behavior, is it to be accepted, liked, or is it simply because you are trying to be a kind human being? To weigh this, take a look at what you feel when you are doing things to please those individuals. Do you ever get frustrated or aggravated? Do you dread having to be in the presence of those people because you know you need to please them.

The next time that you find yourself in this position weigh the facts and if doing something for someone else is outside of the scope of just being a good person versus you pleasing them so that you can be accepted, liked, or to fit in, then maybe you should take a step back and say no not this time.

Do The Work

How often do you find yourself people pleasing?

_____

_____

_____

_____

_____

How does this make you feel?

_____

_____

_____

_____

_____

What changes can you make in the future to ensure that you are only doing things because you want to and not to please someone else?

_____

_____

_____

_____

_____

TODAY'S AFFIRMATION

"Today I choose to say no because I can"

How does it make you feel thinking about saying no to someone when they ask you to do something you do not want to?

_____

_____

_____

_____

_____

Week Three

Day Seven

"Saying no is not a negative thing it is a positive when it establishes your boundaries"

Boundaries are establishing the rules that govern your life in accordance to how much you let people into your space. If you find relationships create more chaos, then care you probably need a boundary. If you find yourself always overly involved in other people's lives because they insert themselves into yours even at the most inopportune times you probably need a boundary.

Creating boundaries can be difficult especially when you must create those boundaries with people that you love however creating those boundaries will create a space of peace for you. Do not allow other people to infiltrate your space they do not bring to you but take from you. Saying no again is not a negative thing, it is a positive thing when you are establishing your boundaries.

Do The Work

Who do you need to set boundaries with?

_____

_____

_____

_____

_____

When thinking about setting boundaries how do you feel?

_____

_____

_____

_____

_____

How will you set boundaries with those individuals?

_____

_____

_____

_____

_____

TODAY'S AFFIRMATION

"Today I choose just say no to negative energy and embrace a positive mindset"

What is the positive mindset that you have set for yourself?

_____

_____

_____

_____

_____

CONCLUSION

CONCLUSION

You have finally come to the end of this book but not the end of your journey. The work continues as you live your day-to-day life. Now the true journey begins as you develop into the person you have purpose to be. As you continue this journey remember not to allow fear to hinder your growth, because when things begin to change it can be scary. Entering uncharted territory can have that effect on you. However, know that you can and will be the best version of yourself if you keep trying.

Hopefully, you have found the courage to break out of the shell that has been holding you back. This book was created to be the catalyst to jump start you on your journey to that freedom. Breaking free is one thing, staying free is another thing. It is now up to you to continue to take the information you have learned here and continuously apply it to your everyday life. Always be intentional about allowing yourself room to keep growing and developing into the version of yourself that is authentic. Do not settle for being a cheap version of someone else but stand in your truth and be an expensive original.

If you find yourself falling back into trying to please other people and not being true to yourself, go back and review the work you have done. Remind yourself of your why, why you chose to break free, why you chose to embrace who you truly are and why it is okay for you to say no. You are the one who controls your life so navigate yourself toward a happier and emotionally healthier you. Stay the course no matter what tries to deter you from your journey.

You are finally free to be you. Remember the lessons you have learned over the past 21 days, you have removed the mask so that you can clearly see who you are, you have taken steps to identify where the problems started with your past identity, and you have done the work to free yourself of that image that others created for you. You have begun to embrace who you are as an individual based on your own rules and no longer trapped by the misconception of who others think you should be. You have begun to reframe how you see yourself, you are no longer looking through the lens of others. Most of all you are learning that saying no and creating healthy boundaries frees you from the people pleasing mentality which can be extremely exhausting.

Continue to seek out your truth as you continue your journey free to be me you are worthy you are smart you are lovable just being who you are. Stay out of the box of others' opinions and walk in the truth of the phenomenal person you are. When you look in the mirror make sure the person looking back at you is the person you desire to be and say to yourself, "I AM FREE TO BE ME UNAPOLOGETICALLY."

Personal
Journal

Free to Be Me Journal

_____

_____

_____

_____

_____

_____

_____

_____

_____

_____

_____

_____

_____

_____

_____

_____

_____

_____

_____

Free to Be Me Journal

_____

_____

_____

_____

_____

_____

_____

_____

_____

_____

_____

_____

_____

_____

_____

_____

_____

Free to Be Me Journal

_____

_____

_____

_____

_____

_____

_____

_____

_____

_____

_____

_____

_____

_____

_____

_____

_____

_____

Free to Be Me Journal

_____

_____

_____

_____

_____

_____

_____

_____

_____

_____

_____

_____

_____

_____

_____

_____

_____

_____

Free to Be Me Journal

_____

_____

_____

_____

_____

_____

_____

_____

_____

_____

_____

_____

_____

_____

_____

_____

_____

_____

Free to Be Me Journal

_____

_____

_____

_____

_____

_____

_____

_____

_____

_____

_____

_____

_____

_____

_____

_____

_____

_____

Free to Be Me Journal

_____

_____

_____

_____

_____

_____

_____

_____

_____

_____

_____

_____

_____

_____

_____

_____

_____

_____

Free to Be Me Journal

_____

_____

_____

_____

_____

_____

_____

_____

_____

_____

_____

_____

_____

_____

_____

_____

_____

_____

_____

Free to Be Me Journal

Free to Be Me Journal

_____

_____

_____

_____

_____

_____

_____

_____

_____

_____

_____

_____

_____

_____

_____

_____

_____

_____

Free to Be Me Journal

_____

_____

_____

_____

_____

_____

_____

_____

_____

_____

_____

_____

_____

_____

_____

_____

_____

_____

_____

_____

_____

Free to Be Me Journal

_____

_____

_____

_____

_____

_____

_____

_____

_____

_____

_____

_____

_____

_____

_____

_____

_____

_____

_____

_____

_____

_____

_____

_____

_____

_____

_____

_____

_____

_____

_____

_____

_____

_____

_____

_____

Free to Be Me Journal

_____

_____

_____

_____

_____

_____

_____

_____

_____

_____

_____

_____

_____

_____

_____

_____

_____

Free to Be Me Journal

_____

_____

_____

_____

_____

_____

_____

_____

_____

_____

_____

_____

_____

_____

_____

_____

_____

_____

Free to Be Me Journal

_____

_____

_____

_____

_____

_____

_____

_____

_____

_____

_____

_____

_____

_____

_____

_____

_____

_____

_____

_____

_____

_____

_____

_____

_____

_____

_____

_____

_____

_____

_____

_____

_____

_____

_____

_____

Free to Be Me Journal

_____

_____

_____

_____

_____

_____

_____

_____

_____

_____

_____

_____

_____

_____

_____

_____

_____

Free to Be Me Journal

_____

_____

_____

_____

_____

_____

_____

_____

_____

_____

_____

_____

_____

_____

_____

_____

_____

_____

_____

_____

Free to Be Me Journal

_____

_____

_____

_____

_____

_____

_____

_____

_____

_____

_____

_____

_____

_____

_____

_____

Free to Be Me Journal

_____

_____

_____

_____

_____

_____

_____

_____

_____

_____

_____

_____

_____

_____

_____

_____

_____

_____

Made in the USA
Columbia, SC
05 November 2022

70384887R00061